ARCHIVE OF THE UNDRESSED

ARCHIVE OF THE
UNDRESSED

POEMS

JEANETTE LYNES

WOLSAK
& WYNN

Cover design: Marijke Friesen
Cover images: istockphoto
Author's photograph: Deb Stagg
Typset in Sabon
Printed by Coach House Printing Company Toronto, Canada

 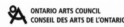

The Canada Council | Le Conseil des Arts
for the Arts | du Canada

ONTARIO ARTS COUNCIL
CONSEIL DES ARTS DE L'ONTARIO

Canadian   Patrimoine
Heritage   canadien

The publisher gratefully acknowledges the support of the Canada Council for the Arts, the Ontario Arts Council and the Canada Book Fund.

Wolsak and Wynn Publishers Ltd.
280 James Street North
Hamilton, ON
Canada L8R 2L3

Library and Archives Canada Cataloguing in Publication

Lynes, Jeanette
    Archive of the undressed / Jeanette Lynes.

Poems.
ISBN 978-1-894987-66-0

    I. Title.

PS8573.Y6A73 2012   C811'.54   C2012-904739-2

Off with that girdle, like heaven's zone glistering,
But a far fairer world encompassing.
Unpin that spangled breastplate which you wear
That th'eyes of busy fools may be stopped there.
Unlace yourself . . .

                              – John Donne

A circle of fine card board and a chance to see a tassel.

                              – Gertrude Stein

CONTENTS

BEGIN THE SLOW PEEL OF
ELBOW GLOVES

The triggering muse for this collection is a stack of vintage *Playboy* magazines I've been immersed in for the past four years. Dating mostly from the 1960s and '70s, these magazines have been my constant travelling companions across our extreme-trek-of-a-country, more than once contributing to overweight baggage charges. It seems the '60s and '70s are now considered "vintage." These magazines' glossy heft and sumptuous contents became for me an archive with a curious staying power. If they fed a fetish, it has been as much for their funky fonts, retro colours, and unfettered period capitalism, as for each issue's highly staged photo shoot of "the girl next door." I read them for the articles, of course! But also the pleasure of *contrast*, juxtaposition – a John Kenneth Galbraith piece beside an ad for Interwoven University Socks in glacier blue, dune grass, wild oats, or buckwood brown. A rousing editorial next to ads for underwear or Harley-Davidsons.

Veiled beneath its script of hedonism and racy "entertainment for gentlemen," *Playboy* has always essentially been a conduct book for men. Its readers could access the regular Advisor column (a kind of reverse-mirror-image Ann Landers) along with the consumer orgy of ads for cars, cologne, whiskey, cigars, clothing, stereos with silky response and party-proof walnut finish, offers of memberships in vinyl record clubs. What to buy. Where to travel. What to cook for romantic dinners. Recipes (booze-laced, surely sponsored by liquor companies). Vintage *Playboy* was a primer on how to pursue the good life. To read it as a woman is to occupy the position of a voyeur – to join a club of voyeurs, as it were, with its transgressive tingle. Gloria

Steinem said, famously, documenting her undercover stint at the Manhattan Playboy Club, "All women are bunnies." It makes you think. But we are also lookers. We like to watch as much as the next guy. As the snaggle-toothed vendor at the Kingston, Ontario, flea market told me when I purchased yet another infusion of vintage *Playboys*, "It's all women that buys them." It makes you think.

Contemporary *Playboy* magazines have little resonance for me; the same goes for keyed clubs or reality TV about Playmates' daily lives at The Mansion. The early decades of *Playboy* are its golden age. Issues from the 1950s are scarce as centrefolds' clothing; the inaugural *Playboy* with Marilyn Monroe on its cover and a price of fifty cents auctions high on eBay. The centrefolds and other visuals from the 1960s hold residual traces of an earlier pin-up era with its aesthetic of visual tease. Vintage Playmate centrefolds were classy, coy. Beginning in the 1970s the magazine's soft aesthetic, its tease, began to give way to visuals that left nothing to the imagination. All strip, no tease. It was all over, for me, by 1980, the year Canadian Playmate Dorothy Stratten was murdered. A tragic signifier who still haunts our collective imagination, Stratten wasn't the only Playmate to suffer a grisly demise; the road to celebrity is littered with Playmates' bodies. I began a tally – three murdered, four overdosed, four car crashes, one plane crash – but after imagining roses for the Playmates, I set aside this morbid ledger and the slow shimmy of these poems moved towards an alternative world of undress. The women who pose for *Playboy* have to share space, inside the covers of this book, with burlesque performers.

Despite the sustained spell vintage *Playboy* cast over me and despite their aesthetic of the tease, the world within these magazines is, ultimately, a milieu malnourished in irony and play. Even the cartoons – perhaps *especially* the cartoons – haven't aged well. There's something isolationist about *Playboy*, something, in the end, *lonely*. Despite the visual continuity from issue to issue, no interviewed Playmate ever references an *earlier* Playmate, her voluptuous predecessor of the gatefold. Each Playmate waxes eloquent (or not) about her hobbies and aspirations but never do we hear her say, "I *so* enjoyed Gaye Rennie's thoughts on bowling last month" (April 1968) or "I found the feature on 'raven-tressed part Choctaw' centerfold Tonya Crews truly absorbing" (March 1961). Each curvaceous body was frozen in time inside the bubble of the month, held within the frame, denuded of context. It's like she alone existed, atomized as a 1950s suburban housewife, nude but for an apron or dust mop flung casually over her lower parts. And not nearly enough tassels. After four years of immersion in vintage *Playboy*, loneliness had had its day.

My thoughts turned towards the social. In the end one can't sit alone and read old *Playboy* magazines forever. I signed up for a burlesque class. As live performance, burlesque differs, of course, from glossy magazine photo shoots. Neo-burlesque is laden with historical gestures, with irony, with references to earlier grand ladies of the stage, the pioneers of undress, icons like Gypsy Rose Lee, Sally Rand, Lili St. Cyr. Neo-burlesque can take the form of homage or tribute to these icons; there's an awareness of history, cultural context, a carny-tinged tradition traceable all the way back to Aristophanes. The Burly World is not without tragedy, to be sure. And traditional burlesque sometimes veered towards the monstrous, the exploitative circus spectacle. Performers often led lonely lives on the road, solitary journeys to the burly gates. More than one burlesque queen died alone in a hotel room. Rhinestone-studded ostrich fans for all the ladies. Yet burlesque, with its connectedness to a performative and satirical tradition and, above all, its *humour*, exerted a reanimating influence and nudged me out of my own dark night. Burlesque is an accommodating space; neither youth nor a particular set of measurements is required for admission to the club. It's gratifying to see neo-burlesque ladies take back the bunny.

The link between *Playboy* and burlesque may seem attenuated as a worn G-string, yet Hugh Hefner, who sprang from rural, Puritan roots, came of age under the romantic spell of the showgirl, of Ziegfeld Follies, the Minsky Brothers, the lavish spectacles of Hollywood. "The girl next door" is a nice trope but it was really the figure of the showgirl who captured Hefner's imagination – a showgirl-waitress with bunny ears and tail. Colonized burlesque. An area of confluence between golden-era *Playboy* and burlesque is the element of tease – that chiffon scarf will never be pulled aside in those vintage centrefolds, those bikini bottoms hang forever half-down. Grecian-Urn Tease, a nod to Keats. Vintage *Playboy* visuals come closest to a burlesque aesthetic. Those old centrefolds are static manifestations of the alluring dancers on a live stage, deferring the reveal.

In Andrew Marvell's famous poem "To His Coy Mistress," the man wants striptease (fast pleasures torn with rough strife). The "mistress" who is addressed but whose response isn't notated directly – there's no real need within the machinations of the poem; we know she's resisting – wants burlesque (slow vegetable love). The contrastive tension pulls the poem tight as corset strings.

To be "undressed" signifies exposure. Exposure can imply vulnerability or spectacle. It has long struck me how society views the female body as public property; the way I've seen people place a hand on a pregnant woman's stomach without asking permission. The way people feel no compunction about shouting comments about the length of my skirt when I'm walking in public in summer. It's like living on a stage, just like Shakespeare said. 'The gaze' never goes off-shift. But I, too, am a gazer. These poems examine bodies, discovered, lost, revealed and hidden, regulated bodies, bodies yielding to their unfettered appetites, aging bodies, framed bodies, kinetic bodies, bodies with reverb, historical bodies, animal bodies, bird bodies, bodies decked in flowers, museum bodies, costumed bodies, gothic bodies, elegized bodies, tragic bodies, comic bodies, tragicomic bodies, obscure bodies, celebrity bodies, local bodies. Bodies situated within the matrix of popular culture, part of which is time-and-place-specific vernacular language.

I mined vintage *Playboy* for the terminology of its era – hence words like "harpy," "knockout," "bird." "The Queen's Bush" was a popular name given, during the pioneer era of Ontario, to the country north of Guelph, in particular, the often-difficult terrain through which Highway 6 was hewn with pickaxe and horse. Canada itself, with its interminable distances and slow reveal, might just have a burlesque heart. I grew up in The Queen's Bush, odd as that sounds – and it's as impossible to pluck my own historical body from those stony fields as it is to extricate those Playmates from their folded paper urns.

Yes you in your argyle sweater Hardwick-crested jacket silver and teak
    cufflinks
precision lighter that strikes up "Dixie" each time you spark your
    Guardsman pipe

You whose slacks are habit forming

Whose interiors refulgently grandiose

You scented with Black Watch shave lotion for 'round the clock
    distinction

You with audio fidelity, discerning ears, woofers tweeters in walnut

You with your electric pencil sharpener your rechargeable flashlight
    fountain pen with exclusive snorkel reloading feature

You with the giant pepper mill   the nimble wits

Whose "Mairzy Doats"

You who surround yourself with walnut
                who cha cha
                who pronounce buttons a bore
                who are too hipster for houndstooth
                too busy for bongo drums

You who appreciate a good crisp lagoon

Who demand close shaves

You purveyor of midnight suppers in midtown with stainless steel steak
    knife sets in walnut cases collapsible silver-plated cups

You with your chafing dishes your Yashica Lynx camera with
diaphragm-shutter-coupled electric eye

You with no patience for bothersome antediluvian holdovers

You who prefer to make like a bunny

You who have made four equilateral triangles from cigarettes

You whose party yacht is called *The Mayflower*

You on daylight savings time (Cartier ultra-thin evening watch)

Yes you, with time to watch
                            I'm talking to you –

(November 1967)

Mary-Ann sends up autumn in smoke, puffs on a filter-tipped cigar.
Her father, a Bible teacher.

She broke the state record for the backstroke
at age eleven. Of water, she says –
When I'm submerged I let myself go –

When not submerged she's in a darkroom, photography
a passion. She unwinds
in her bachelorette pad to music, The 5th Dimension –
They can really flip me out.

Her radial chorine-slubbed Burbank nipples evoke sand dollars
known, in some parts of the world, as sea biscuits.

(June 1968)

Brit loves America, is here for keeps.
Serving at a Nordic-style diner on a Minnesota lake
she heard about bunny-ing. The long ears enhanced her
blonde and everyone was so nice.

She's learning English in leaps and sounds. People teach her
more than books, she told *Playboy*. She'd never
be comfortable with anything made of plastic.
That's why we love Brit, she's so natural and if you rise
early you might catch her nude Scandinavian body free
of ears and tail roaming the Los Altos hills
before she hits the library in her plaid suspenders.

(May 1969)

Riding runs in Sally's family, her mother a retired
equestrian instructress. Wearing the bunny tail
feels natural as jumping hurdles
in the pleasure-horse class, says our
blue-ribbon beauty. Her trophies shine
on the mantle at her Central Park pad, friends
wait there with flaming crepe Suzettes.

Sally rides. Sally reads – *my mind will wither
if I don't keep it exercised.*

Sally almost earned a Ph.D. –
instead she artificially inseminated hens on a kibbutz.

She plays autoharp like June Carter.

Cooks French.
Cooks French.

(February 1972)

P. J. Lansing in Boulder

College town. Trendy shops. No urban problems. Miss February
moves among this perfection. A sophomore, major in fashion retail.
Here she models a fur coat open to expose one breast.
Now only a billow of pink blankets around her skin.

Figure, ground.

She's macrobiotic. See her stroll the high country, her mind
rapt with seaweed.

Turn the page – in this shot she's exercising her mouth
for a frat party.

IMAGINARY LETTER FROM THE PEOPLE TO
THE EARLY *PLAYBOY* CENTREFOLDS

Ladies,

We wish to know where all that beauty landed you, what befell after
the glue loosed, gatefolds collapsed, staples unhooked. We have a
right to ride the curvy roads of your flesh to their logical terminuses
it's *our* map, too. We paid good money, now give us the full circus,
almighty blight of neck-wattles, pores curdled and lost, nipples dull
as pennies on tracks after the train long passed.
We want to see you kiss the skids –

hit rock bottom, scrounge and sink straight to the dogs and by the
way which breed do you now resemble most? Who did you think
you were? Look how you cower behind sunglasses, beneath shredded
silk scarves. Oh, wasted stars in your mildewed planets, your
rattletrap fannies slushy as jellied salad left in the sun, your coy-
mistress smiles, let's see the definite article, the shrivel and slump, the
ghoulish, haunted girls.

Signed, The People

Her body: missing. She agrees to talk with one string
attached: they do not show her as she looks now. She is
voice, rasp of pickled oatmeal with a drawl, ancient tart,
a chugging citation of scripture. God has no problem
with nudity, she decrees, consider Garden One.
She pretended the cameras were boyfriends
for whom she lolled and licked and flicked
those notches and nicks in her arty bangs
(scissored by one of history's great lost hairdressers).

She prates through the parade of her old poses.
Laughs a grand total of once, old-flirt guffaw;
She only started to fall apart a couple of years ago.
Now she's sound waves, sonic chop. Sole employee
of both Hugh Hefner and Billy Graham. She's earned
the right to not make sense. To insist the curtain
remain closed. To say when. The centre cannot fold.

The old grey mare ain't who she used to be –
surprised it all devolves to elegy,
to body? Don't be, there's always a body,
missing or not. Lovely or less.
Historic. Histrionic. Hysterical.
Lost in space or not. Girlish. Ghoulish.
Shot to death and swarmed by ants
or not. Either way, the world
wishes to view and will pay.
Disappointed, they'll request a refund.
It's a very exacting world
in the body department and never
over easy, always hard.
Waist knot, want knot.
Body is poultry, so many cartons of eggs.
Dairy. Milk. Mare. Mummy. Centre. Fold.

Tiny evening wear, bevy of wide-eyed dolls.
I have those dolls to thank. They were my first school.
The dolls got bigger, could talk, swivel on stage.
Want to hear a secret? I love sequins

more than sex! I like ruching more than, *you* know.
But my husband I *do* owe, for taking me on his
vice squad rounds, for asking, "Can't you sew
some little bits to keep those girls out of jail?"

Pasties and G-strings financed my house.
Another arcane remnant – fishing-rod swivels
stitched into the pasties twirled the tassels,
on the right lady, faster than a carnival

wheel. Crystal. Horsehair. Netting. Nothing
I wouldn't use in my costumes. It was for the art,
you see (and yes, to keep the artists prison-free).
A well-rendered pleat is more pleasing to me

than sun-threaded rays over backlit surf.
But it was lining, yes, *lining*, that brought the watchers
to their knees. The slow roll of the hand to reveal
the red satin inside, the black brocade

the great jewels of the inner country.
Like all beauty it had to end. Like all flesh, devolve.
First went their tops, half my livelihood right there.
Then their bottoms, other half. Now fishing rods
are used only for fishing. What a waste.

What a waist.

Nobody calls me Ada but my mother and the FBI.
  – Zorita

Orson Welles liked her snakes, Elmer and Oscar.
Truth was they weren't much use, sluggish,
slept in a sack in her closet. Even on stage
they were stupid, half-stunned, no work ethic
at all and she had to lasso them about, feign
terror. All the heavy lifting belonged to her.
A congressman gave her a fox fur. She winked,
later sewed it into a G-string. Marlene Dietrich
praised her sewing prowess, the zing in her
stage name. *Zor-ee-ta.* A bricklayer bricked her house
for free, just to play a part in history.
Zorita loves her scrapbooks, all her pretty girls
under the Christmas tree, alight in black lace.

HOW THE HISTORY OF *PLAYBOY* RESEMBLES
THE HISTORY OF CANADIAN POETRY

Last century deep in the night a young man chuffed with ideals,
stapler in hand, toils at a kitchen table. The damned magazine came
out backwards so he yanks the staples. No one knows better than
him if you want it done right you must do it yourself, wait, he *did*
do this himself. He's had to borrow cash from his mother, among
others, to print it. He must work quietly. His wife is asleep, she does
not approve. Doesn't even want to know, only knows she does not
approve, won't forgive him for selling a few pieces of their few pieces
of furniture to buy paper for this silly dream he chases leaving them
with sticks and next thing she knows he'll quit his day job *then* what
will they do it will be all up to her and it's not like
she enjoys slugging it out on the candy assembly line the syrup smell
sickens her especially in her current condition but *some*one must
keep them afloat *some*one must be practical all he does is draw
cartoons and bluster he'll show the square world what's what his
magazine will trigger a revolution change society as we know it if
only those damned staples hold. He's sure he'll be an urban legend
soon enough oh *ho ho* soon enough *diapers* are what he'll change
and she's scared some morning she'll come downstairs and the
toaster will be gone he'll stop at nothing to make his magazine he'll
even sacrifice sleep and toast. If only he could banish her voice from
his head its constant jangle distracts and the work would advance
more quickly without that censorious wail like some siren crane fly
in his entrepreneurial ears.

Possible Name: Puck Bunny; Possible Subtitle: Overtime for Men

Possible Logo: Antlers (?)

Possible Feature Articles:

The Country's Best Doughnuts

Ten Turbo Brews to Keep You on the Road

Bud for a Hot Bod

Has Poutine Replaced Sex?

Has Ikea Replaced Sex?

Has Knitting Replaced Sex?

Has Thinking Replaced Sex?

How Much is too Much?

Fame in Canada: You *Know*, What's-'Er-Name, You *Know*, Whatcha-Ma-Hooey

Where to Buy the Best Block Heater

Confessions of a Go-Go Girl in Love with Someone Who Didn't Care

Should You Give Her Snow Tires for Christmas?

The New Ski-Doos

Can Leonard Cohen Still Cut It in Bed?

Ten New Beers Sure to Score

Secret Paul Anka Sex Ring Discovered Years Later

Travel:

Newfoundland's Best Nudist Colonies (Of Unrequited Dreams)

Getaway Weekends in Fort McMurray

At long Last – A Peek Under the Kilts of Nova Scotia: Does it Rise
to all the Mac-Hype?

Value Village, The New Hot Dating Spot

Polygamy on Two Dollars a Day

The Arctic's Little Vegas

Centrefold Pitches:

What She Looks Like Without Her Toque

Parkas Away (visual: someone slitting open a parka, two nude
bodies obscured by a blizzard of down feathers)

Why it's Sexy as Hell When She Drinks from the Carton

The New Distressed Scarves, Games with Earmuffs

Other Possible Features:

Readers Vote – Canada's most Well-Endowed Lady
(Note: approach CBC, check out possible grant programs)

Long Johns Silver

Why Figure Skaters are Icy in Bed

Trudeau, Canada's Last Swinger

Justin Bieber, A Reverse-Lolita?

More Recipes for Vegetable Sex

Sample Advisor Columns:

Dear Advisor,
I have been seeing a fine lady for nearly a year and the "L" word
has been floated a few times. But she has the most annoying habit of
leaving her empty Tim Hortons cups strewn all over the floor of my
pickup truck. Over time I think this unpleasant habit could drive a
wedge between us. Sadly, the lady is a slob. What should I do?
Signed, Fed Up With Bad Truck Etiquette

Dear F. U.,
Your lady's Tim's-cup habit spells future disaster. Float the "F"
word one last time – Get out while the coffee's still fresh in the cup!
Buy her a large double-double if that's what it takes.
Signed, Advisor

Dear Advisor,
My wife and I still have a sex life after sixteen years of marriage.
But she continues to remain a loyal Toronto Maple Leafs fan even
though, the day I proposed, she promised she'd quit this delusional
path and cheer for my team. She doesn't even sneak off and root for

the Leafs. She brazenly hoots and cheers them on behind the closed door of her study (needless to say these game nights are not sex nights for us). I love her but it's really eating at me that she hasn't left her Leaf addiction behind like she promised years ago. I don't know how much longer I can live with a woman who can't keep her word.

Signed, Leaf-Blight in Terrace Bay

Dear Blight on the Terrace,

Take control. Toss her television into Lake Superior! Tell her enough is enough. It's your way or the highway.

Signed, Advisor

Dear Advisor,

My boyfriend insists on wearing a Canada Post uniform to bed. He sewed it himself. It's very convincing. The problem is it's such an incredible turn-on I climax even before things get interesting. What should I do?

Signed, Ken in Kitsilano

Dear Ken in Kits,

We've heard everyone loves a man in uniform but this is one gelastic situation you're in. Put another way, it's a good problem you've got, Ken. We say to you, the male must get through! PS: If only the *real* mail came as fast.

Signed, Advisor

Other Approaches:
Look into possible partnerships with curling clubs across the country re: club franchise.

END NOTE: The grant proposal for this magazine was turned down because while the jury scored it high on Canadian content, it tanked on gravity.

HUGH HEFNER, BOY

To dumb animals please be kind –
the message of his childhood poems. His mother
marvelled at his artistry, that tadpole of hers,
his drawings – flying men in capes, cowboys.
Outlaws. This is how the west was won, he told
himself, along with *real* boys. What a world –
visionaries, pinochle, potlucks.
Paradise peopled with clay figurines –
many bore a striking resemblance
to Bela Lugosi. He'd make them tell
stories. All those boys need entertainment.
As for the figures, they'd do whatever
he told them. From this dream of clay . . .

(Expo '67)

While I waited in the Lost Children's Centre
to be claimed, shame coursing the core
of my muddled limbs, my ears
befuddled by Canada's other official tongue
that on this island (eel) failed to echo my morning
show with the mouse puppet and pretty girl

the clown thrust his enormous bulb
nose into my wayward tear-wet face,
strove to divert me with bilingual
balloons torqued into critters with accents
and while I reckoned I took a wrong turn
back at *Man And His World*, last saw my folks
near the giant globe silvered and trussed
like some tinsel planet or vast glass marble
I realized I was who I was: Orphan. Stray.
Stupid. Lost. Girl.

And while the state of being rudderless
in an amusement theme park
built for nationalism hit me deepest
in my girl parts, somewhere else
someone was paging through the latest *Playboy*
where bodies floated free of gravity:
a man in a blue suit, woman with waved
glossy hair, floral billowing dress,
planet Earth below
Smirnoff Skyballs in their hands
they look pleasured to the point of delirium –
    – *Nothing more delicious on earth* –

Near them, an astronaut adrift
with a fat basketball head, silver
like the haloed stadium
where last I saw my folks.

Truth was, I was a *bit old* to be lost.

How I longed to not have a body

                                        above all stray one

to float free

as Smirnoff.

Wink broadly and think of the land. The land will teach you. Think
how hard won, every single mile. Think snail crawl, dawdle and
tease, slowest road trip known to man. Think "are we there yet."
Indeed we are *not* there yet. We won't arrive for a very long time.
Lower your fur-studded parka one fur-hair at a time. Slug it down
embog and lick your lips. Remember the highway's long waistband.
Imagine the country as a huge skirt made of cloth panels hooked
to the waistband, many hooks, a day between each hook. Make
each unhooking a ritual moment, like stopping for gas. Unhook
once at each gas stop. One skirt-panel dropped in the parking lot
near the fuel tanks, left there to tease the unknown traveller or the
service-station attendant or whoever stumbles on it. Leave a trail
of skirt-panels across the country. Banners of your glacial dance. If
you discover feathers or bits of antler or rabbit fur on the ground at
your gas stops make them part of your outfit. You're allowed some
improvisational space to breathe. Within limits. The time it takes
to drive around Lake Superior's wolfish mane should equate to the
rolling down of one long velvet glove yes that slow. Do not stop in
Thunder Bay. You will only get into trouble there. This sounds like a
lot of rules but it's not. Swirl the glove high in the air then toss it out
the window into a patch of muskeg. Assume the westbound position.
Gaze out the window. The land is your audience. Study the fence
tops poking through snow, tiaras fashioned from barbed weather.
Finger the feathers, the bits of antler. Picture the crashing bucks, the
blowout brawl that must have severed that antler. Wink. Indeed we
are not there yet. We won't arrive for ages. Blow kisses to the last
few remaining old codgers at the one-horse coffee stop. What the
hay, why not leave the other glove there, draped over a clump of oil-
singed sage? That would make some codger's day. By the time you
tour your act back through here those old ones will have vanished.
Give them one last thrill then wane your pace. Do not pause in
Calgary to get tattooed. Remain alert. It behooves you to stay awake
otherwise your mascara will smudge before British Columbia and

you will resemble a harlot. You're not a harlot. You are an artist.
Part of a lineage zagging back to Ziegfeld's Follies. A broad way, a
border-crossed gangling road with much less light and no you are
not there yet. Only when the switchbacks begin and another day and
night wearing slow-motion roller skates derbies down to the coast
and its storybook firs might you consider the sequins on your bust,
how you'll emerge at last through veils of coastal mist from a giant
seashell to tsunamis of applause, cheers and stamping feet, standing
ovations, the land brought to its knees, the teacher taught.

There isn't one of us who hasn't left a piece of our clothing in
  Thunder Bay.

I told you not to stop in Thunder Bay, weren't you listening?

Yes I caught that. But we're not a people who follow instructions well –

all too often our eyes clog with sequin dust.

What I have learned about life –

you just nicely get your clothes off and it's time to go.

Carnivals figure throughout our lives. Farmers' market, row upon row
of puffed wheat squares. Yonge Street on either side, either century.
The office Halloween party. Any textile boom. All those times
they lured you in with a joke.
The time you ran away from home to the Calgary Stampede.
The Royal Winter Fair's lady carved from butter.
The epic English Ferris wheel from which, expounded
the brochure, you can see clear to Canterbury. Like hell the pilgrims
were on their way to pray.
The Wife of Bath with her big bustling skirts, storied spouses.

(*Playboy*, June 1980)

About lip gloss they were never wrong, the old bastards
shooting roll after roll, their lenses in love with Dorothy Stratten's
Dairy Queen smile. Even now her lips
glow though she's been breathless a trio of decades, butterfly
still parked on her pictorial wrist, its wings lit like tawny stained glass.
This is the last innocent cover and everyone wanted it to happen.
Her gauze top poised to fall (but won't).
We called those peasant blouses.
To dress like a cropper or serf was the rage, then.

Deep inside the pages, Dorothy's pelt, startlingly dark,
as ours often were (peroxide our fetish *above* the neck,
schisms were us). Girls got discovered. It could have been
any Dairy Queen. Death likes frozen treats
much as anyone, girls in uniform cranking the soft
ice cream machine. The cosmic dice spat their dots
down on Coquitlam. Death ordered a hot fudge sundae.
Beamed at Dorothy, his gold neck-chain glinting, he snapped
her picture. She'd be his rocket to the moon.

She fell into an ocean that day and no one noticed.
Playboy was too busy adoring her, dubbing her life
a fairy tale. Quoting her ambition –
to be surrounded by pets –
(a girl could claim this back then and remain
valid in everyone's eyes). See her, still chaste
in pink leg warmers. Topless as the girl next door.
Now she tosses the ball to a puppy that doesn't
see she's undressed, also how they found her
shot dead. Nude. No puppy. Only construction crews of ants
dragging red bridges across her chilled bare back,

working to rule. Building blood colonies
across that *other* body, too, the one from Dairy Queen,
pistol a stiff extension of his husband-hand.

After some hours so *many* ants, the corpses
resolved into dark, rolling waves on a starless sea
of no return and somewhere an evergreen forest
was flinging its seeds and I, in college denim buttoned
to the neck, was opening a window.

There's always a body.

The Mansion swells with desolation. Nobody's there, we sing. And moan, as our bones ache, our mind rages with thoughts of beauty, and destruction.
  – Lynn Crosbie

At all times have I lived shooting distance from some mansion. Casa Loma. Victoria College (spinning past on my bike, cigarette in hand – hedonist cyclist). Banff Springs Hotel, briefly. The Mansion in Kingston (shambling roadhouse tinged with rumours of celebrity, sin). Kingston Pen, red turreted roof like the castle kicking off *The Wonderful World of Disney.* Childhood's dusted road, a fancy farm not far from ours, an Agrarian Graceland, the Joneses no one could keep up with, their hacienda obscured by poplar thickets, scandal – *They got their money from betting at the racetrack, imagine.* Dirty derbies, who knew what else? Our minds thread-narrow. Hindsight lacked progressive lenses. *The wife has a fur coat, I saw her at the IGA, imagine.* Even the Joneses needed groceries. At the mansion lived a girl with dazzling teeth. She rode the school bus with the rest of us. We distrusted anyone with dental work. Her home had the only in-ground swimming pool for miles around. That's how we knew that place was a Babylon hive. That's why I had to see it for myself. The daughter was lonely. She invited me to her mansion. Pool. I pretended I could swim, got reeled out by the scruff of my life yet even gasping, flailing, the aqua evanescence closing in on me I could glimpse the rose gardens with their opulent butterflies and if you had to die it should be beautiful at least.

Once upon a time, according to my father, two monsters ruled the
world:
   1. Big Business
   2. Goddamn Trudeau
They were in cahoots. We were doomed on our little farm. Then
there was God. God sent hail. The corn buckled and tore. The
zucchinis smouldered with bruises. Letters arrived from Big Business
– *you are tiny* – *as a matter of fact you will disappear any day now.*
Hellfire and rhinestone.
No wonder I traded my reason for magazine spreads, headlines.
I *liked* Pierre's buckskin jacket, solid teeth, flower-child wife. At that
austere shrinking juncture she was a glimpse of possibility within a
northern context. I clipped their wedding picture, blossoms strewn
so artfully through her hair you'd swear

they'd seeded there.
She showed me a future – garden tresses, higher learning (she'd been
to university). Liberalism. Glamour. Bring me flowers and hairpins!
I renamed my bedroom *boudoir* – whenever my mother referenced
it, as in "tidy that bedroom of yours," I countered, *I know not what
you mean, I'm not acquainted with any such room – it's no longer
on the map of this house!*

In the chamber formerly known as my bedroom I filled my hair with
blossoms. I told my dolls stories. Whatever I said, they believed, even
the crack-eyed one. I'm sure it was the flowers. I wished my dolls a
happy doll-hood.

And that's how the petals spun through Mrs. Trudeau's dark lovely
hair kept me from disappearing. Margaret, botanical bride with a
brain.

Dear Archivist Poet or Whoever You Purport to be: I am disappointed. I thought this book would be fun to read. You have a reputation for being quirky and humorous. But much of this is morbid reaching over to depressing.

Dear Reader: I am sorry for seducing your hopes or derailing your expectations but not *that* sorry and cannot assume full blame as poetry, whether stripped down or dressed as prose, cannot always be the opiate of the pupil.

I suggest you go bite my cottontail.

Farmers. Marquis de Sodbusters. Yep that was us. The stony land
demanded a dominant stance. Each season it had to be shown who
was boss. Ruled with an iron brand (Massey-Harris), heavy dose
of diesel. Crop rotation. The groundhogs punching holes in the
fields to fashion their underground mansions where no doubt furry
orgies occurred, debauches like in that painting by Bosch only with
groundhogs. Those crazed tunnel-sinners must be put in their place,
enter the township boys with their pellet rifles, *thwack thwack
kapow*, sound balloons just like in the funnies. You thought we bore
no arms?[1] Point of historical fact. The Queen's Bush was once a
region of great lawlessness, witness the 1859 shootout at Campbell's
Tavern, dispute over some horses *kaboom* up in smoke. Ours was
a long covert tradition of firearms. Aggressive passive. But in truth
neither musket nor flintlock nor peashooter was our finest form.
Our element was: rope, whip, strap, hog-knot. In this hardware
we shone our brightest. The Northern Academy of Discipline and
Pun(ish). Mannish. Clan(ish). *The rawhide whip and the tawse (a
long leather strap split into strips) were the only instruments used
for punishment by Master Gamble. His predecessor in the school – a
man named Fitzpatrick – had been noted for his floggings. A stout
lad was chosen, whose shoulders had to be mounted by the culprit,
and whose wrists had to be firmly grasped by the mounter. Then
with beech gads the master laid on with vigour upon the back and
buttocks of the victim until fatigue or the giving out of the beech
gads called a halt to the proceedings. Strange to say, in those early
days both parents and trustees were firmly of the opinion – chiefly,
I suppose, because in their own school days they had undergone
similar forms of education – that knowledge was chiefly instilled
by the gad. So much was this the case that trustees would, if
possible, hire a teacher who had a reputation for giving "sound
thrashings."*[2] A gad! A goad! A spike a prod. Imagine being noted
for your floggings, to go down in history on that note. Marquis de
Fitzpatrick.

How soft grew our educations! Take me, growing up at the end
of things, a ripple far from the centre. Like Canada itself, a kind
of aftershock of America. Grade two, last one-room schoolhouse
in the township, our young mistress and her wood-notched ruler
(imperial inches) mostly symbolic, more empty threat than red fanny
(we did not say "buttock"). Or brandishing the fly swatter when the
swatting part flew across the map of the world. Not even the flies
were afraid in those days of S & M Lite, the stones largely subdued
into heaps or marshalled into fences and the new Marquis had not
yet arrived, Marquis de Monsanto, his hardware gone vaporous,
chemical, corporate. *Whoosh kapow* the master lay on with vigour.
Groundhog Day could not last forever.[3]

---

[1] Unlike our pistol-whipping neighbours to the south we did not flash our
firearms or hang them from our belts or trucks (aggressive aggressive O say
can you see). Ours we stashed passive behind the hi-fi where Karen Carpen-
ter's vinyl voice made its hungry laps around and around.

[2] W. M. Brown, *The Queen's Bush: A Tale of the Early Days of Bruce
County* (London, ON: John Bale, Sons & Danielsson, Ltd, 1932).

[3] Note the inherently submissive position of footnotes.

He parks his ancient Buick on the main drag,
Princess Street, near banks, cafés,
a stone's toss from S & R Department Store
with its living elevator operator who resembles
a dead Bee Gee. Yes, the oldest swinger
in Canada brakes his buggy buffed with love
amidst all this glamour. Weather means zilch to him.
I first saw him on winter's most dire day, walkers
picking their way along Bagot, muttering prayers
into their scarves. His Buick equipped with state-
of-the-art eight-track, windows wide open,
Glenn Miller or Artie Shaw full tilt. I was about to tell
a mental health professional nothing good
remained in this world when I noted
the nation's oldest living swinger,
his passion pit parked, big band cranked,
his bald head tilted back, joggling
to the riffs. His eyes closed,
mouth open, gums aglow,
pink galleries of pure bliss.

The hymnal era had ended. Presbyterian fires goodbye. College hello.
North York. Holy holy holy. An uncharted lewdness to the south:
downtown. Things will be great
when you're. Frosh week's libertine colour scheme. Residence life.
Roxy Music. I grew new body parts the day I walked through that
door. Seven days of wet T-shirt contests, undergarments thrown from
windows, snagged in branches.

HOW HUGH HEFNER'S PARENTS BEGAN THE SEXUAL REVOLUTION IN NEBRASKA

A boy. A girl. A Methodist dance.

He walks her home   through nodding wild onion

columbine   fescue and brome

jointgrass   columbine

tumbling thistle

                    sticky cockle (seriously)

An Indigo Dusk butterfly flirts past them.

Her parents warned, be back before ten.

She thinks it's funny how everything

can keep growing in the dark, the thistle

keep tumbling   fescue, brome

Rescue, home.

Read it like an honest man, linear, one page then the next.
Or an honest woman, girdled with scrutiny, one boxing glove
stuffed inside each bra cup. Read it with restraint, muster
your resolve! Get hold of yourself! Don't cheat and flip
to the centrefold (we all know what the centre holds,
booty always buried in polite society) – besides, you read it
for the articles, right? Read it like a sentimentalist, dew-eyed,
recalling why the gifts remain wrapped beneath the tree
long before Christmas, why good things come to those
who wait. Read it like a marathon runner, pace yourself
for that final burst to the centre. Read it like Aristotle,
beginning, middle, end, the perfect pleasure arc.
Read it like a Puritan, don't laugh at the cartoons.
Read it like a latter-day Utah dude, adoring wives flanking
your armchair. Read it alone while you sneak a cigar
in a silk smoking jacket no one knows you own
or a chiffon dress like Klinger on *M*A*S*H*.
Read it like the US Army. Or don your studded collar.
Or read it like a Canadian, with coffee and doughnuts.
Read it as a mechanic, building the crankshaft
of your dreams, like the beauty in the ad
before the centrefold, *The Vibration Tamer*,
each cheek and rod and pin in place.
Never lose sight of the centre of rotation.
Read it with a method, a method
will keep you on the up and up.
Every reader needs a method.

And really all this
has been about life
on the outside

I liked to walk up Fifth Avenue
and pick out romantic women
from the crowd and imagine that
in a few minutes I was going to enter
their lives, and no one would ever
know or disapprove. Sometimes,
in my mind, I followed them
to their apartments on the corners
of hidden streets, and they turned
and smiled back at me before they
faded through a door into warm

about being alone

darkness. At the enchanted
metropolitan twilight I felt a

petals on a wet,
black bough

haunting loneliness sometimes,
and felt it in others – poor young
clerks who loitered in front of
windows waiting until it was time

verb-less

for a solitary restaurant dinner –
young clerks in the dusk, wasting
the most poignant moments of night
and life . . . imagining that I, too,
was hurrying towards gaiety and
sharing their intimate excitements,
I wished them well.

rendered Nordic,
Prufrock in a toque

I liked to walk up Yonge Street
and pick out off-duty exotic dancers
from the crowd and imagine that
in a few minutes I was going to enter
their lives, and no one would ever
know or disapprove. Sometimes,
in my mind I followed them
to their subsidized housing units

on the corners of hidden streets
and they turned and glared at me
before they faded through a door
into frigid dark to cook Kraft Dinner.
At the accursed bleak dusk I felt a
haunting loneliness sometimes,
and felt it in others – goalies,

lonely men
in plaid shirt sleeves

laid-off postal workers who loitered
in front of Fran's Restaurant
until it was time for a solitary
supper of pancakes – young auditors
riding the subway, wasting
the most boring moments of night
and life . . . imagining that I, too,
was hurrying towards televised
sports and sharing their intimate
excitement, I wished them well.

brittle bawl of lake gull,
new century

I liked to walk up Princess Street
in Kingston with others not incarcerated
and pick out military personnel
from the crowd and imagine that
in a few minutes I was going to enter
their compounds, and no one
would ever know or disapprove.
Sometimes, in my mind, I followed
them to the apartments of absent
women where they rifled through

winged scavengers
will Dumpster dive
for a mere kernel

lingerie drawers on the corners
of hidden streets, and they turned
and shrugged at me before
they faded through a back gusset
under satin moonlight. At the illicit
Loyalist last call I felt a haunting
loneliness sometimes, and felt it
in others – pitiable young petty

officers who lingered in roadhouses
until it was time for a solitary
burger special – young wardens
in the panopticon's hard ray,
wasting the most incriminating
moments of

night (shift) and life and
                    no one

would ever know

or disapprove.

A ROSE FOR YVETTE VICKERS (1928–2010 OR 2011)

She had a suitcase, terrific tresses. The White Rain Girl.
White Rain, guaranteed not to dull or dry your hair.
Compact as a firecracker on Independence Day.
Star material. Honey Parker in *Attack of the 50 Foot Woman.*
Cast by Cagney in *Short Cut to Hell.* Then Hefner
as Miss July 1959. Being stalked made her screams
in *Attack of the Giant Leeches* highly authentic.
She grew gothic, monstrous, chaste. Withdrew
behind locked gates, Benedict Canyon, was not home.
Was home. That was the worst of it.
Her fan mail cobwebbed, crammed in the box
said her neighbour who scaled the wall at last,
Hello? Hello, found Miss July.
Reporters went crazy for the word *mummified.*
Dead possibly a year. Swallows swooped
through roof-rents in her dilapidated mansion.
White rain. Playmate with no one to play with.
Recluse. Mummy. Victim of giant leeches.
Miss July.

When Miss Yvette Vickers died no one noticed.

To be that alone

You traded down – now you're a clown,
flap and shimmy in the gutter.
Old cigar smoke your new gown.
You used to dance – damask uptown.
You traded down, you clown,
prancing dog, sad-girl-pirate. Strutter,
you traded down. Now be the clown,
flapper. Shimmy in the gutter!

The land denuded, surveyed & carved: concession, lot, back forty,
    baseline &
even bigger boxes of dirt: township, county. Jurisdiction. Fieldwork
after dark, tractor headlights metal-rimmed brassieres burrowing
into the night.
Full. Throttle.

Before that, horses. Voluptuous rumps. Harness & fetlock & shank.
    Fetish.
Working girls. *Giddup. Girl.* Always one mare rose legendary above
all others, a real showgirl, her stamina for fieldwork heretofore
unknown in The Queen's Bush, gnarled frontier hacked north
from Toronto.

They would talk about that one horse, celebrity mare, county
centrefold, years after her death. Extol how she'd a mind of her own
yet no one came close to her for work.

Oral sect.

I've never been a horse person. Yet I imagine the original centrefold mare, *mind of her own*, withers and pastern caked with exertion and mud, farmer like my father and his and his, behind the plough. I fail to fixate on the men.

Rather, the working animal.

The raw, turned furrow in her wake, her, all trussed and strapped

trailing a long dirt boa.

Hindsight is plenty, plenty. A long dirt boa, a trail, the Garafraxa Road's kinked two-hour southbound jounce to Toronto. My first boyfriend (we'd not yet *done it*), me, Lake Ontario's shore, night, unsullied moon unspooling, his finger jabbing at a vast clutch of light across the water – *The States*. No one said America. Always: *The States*. My first sighting sent me into geo-gasm right there on the spot. Later I realized this was a perfectly normal Canadian reaction. Later I understood that glow on the far shore, Hugh Hefner's nightlight.

Are you surprised the original centrefold was a horse? Why should you be? Gulliver fell for a horse and he'd been all over the world – you'd think he'd know. Captain. Explorer. Playboy in foreign lands.

Old Canada, antiquarian books, maximum-security.
The city snowplow in the shop. Perfect day for *Playboy*,
glass of port, pipe. Imagine a pipe. John Kenneth Galbraith looks
like Boris Karloff (Hefner's idol). Galbraith says everyone
in the CIA wants to be James Bond, get all the beautiful women.
The Girls of Scandinavia, pure sensuality despite the harsh climate.
Copenhagen, *a lush hunting ground.*
All you have to do is scribble "Kunne De taneke Dem en drink?"
(How about a drink?) on a napkin. Of working women: *the
inquiring traveller might find himself in the company of a lovely
kindergarten teacher or a sweet-faced secretary using this ancient
means to augment her income.* They've perfected the welfare state.
Swedish girls like to tinker with their sports cars. Enjoy fencing and
discotheques. They dream of New York, look nothing like
Boris Karloff unless
you wish it. Married women vacation alone and unlike the wives of
America aren't the least bit jealous. Norwegian girls: more serious
but get them out on a hike, they go crazy. Throw in an open hearth,
make it mythic. Scandinavia, egalitarian to the core, they'll stop
at nothing to please their partners. If you want to be called Bond,
James Bond, all you need to do is ask.
Imagine a pipe.

THINKING OF YOU DURING SECURITY SCREENING AT
CALGARY AIRPORT

My bra sets off the alarm –
shocking bosom!
Love, you'd laugh at the serious
Official wanding my chest,
you know, my criminal holder,
limp and harmless
as an old basset hound,
a sports bra with metal grommets,
cross-tab for clipping on a pager
or song device, I suppose
though I'd hardly know –
the only jogging I've done
is to your gate.

I'm not secure –
When I arrive
unhook me,
toss the cotton hound
high – across the room.

'She's not dead, she's English', was once the Procrustean punch line
to half a dozen medieval saws describing the legendary immobility
of the beleaguered British bedmate; it no longer applies. Sexual
dalliance in today's London demands not vivification but downright
stamina. Like they say, London swings, and so do its birds.
  – Playboy, December 1966

These birds can bonk. No longer do they lie back
recalling the Queen. Her majesty doesn't enter
the equation. Bring your bumbershoot,
snag a lass stranded in rain and she'll stare
wet and agog at your fine American suit. Soon
you'll witness her minus miniskirt
and by God's cross she's not dead, nor is she
a royalist – rather, a dancer in discotheques.
Learn to speak Street – "bird sanctuary"
holds new meaning, here. Plunge right in –
We don't believe the trans-Atlantic time lag
will damp your stamina. You are a man of iron,
an intrepid bloke on holiday. Any nightspot
you enter, George Harrison probably owns.
Set your sights on some bird, call her a dead ringer
for Jeanie Shrimpton, *you're in*, Mate!
If things look reversed to you, like cars on roads,
consider it normal. Same with polka-dot
bell-bottoms. That clerk in his silk hat you may
think Procrustean is hurrying to jugged hare
steeped in port, served by a supple limey bunny,
lime stabbed through each nipple. Yeah, I know! –
Crazy! It's eat all night long, best Dover sole
you've ever had and when you call *Wench!*
she appears. This would never happen in America,
taxidermic country of stuffed birds. Of *course* you never
want to go home. No one ever *does.*

Hurtled his roadster straight through the great books
of his country, never once stopped for gas or swerved
to avoid a rabbit. Tore along the spines of Faulkner past
Hemingway's huffing bulls then slowed at last
to flick an affectionate yet manly wave Huck's way,
hell of a kid, that rebel heart, refusal to stay caged
in a world ruled by Aunt Pollys, they formed
an unofficial congress. Sail on, boy. A lusty wind
beat in from the west, one stiff breeze linked
to another like a line of chorus girls in red heels.
His cracking fast car was a Triumph in the latest
series of Triumphs. He throttled it
open, burnt up the interstate, hightailed it.
Left Aunt Polly's bloomers flapping
on the clothesline, sad flag of defeat.

He was no bean-shooter, no dope fiend,
no bindle-punk. Just a hep cat with healthy hungers.
Regular citizen with dreams of berries and bim.

THE PASSIONATE PHOTOGRAPHER TO HIS SUBJECT,
MISS MAY

Come pose for me, then be my bunny
And I will make you pots of money.
We'll never leave the mansion grounds;
Forget about your mother's frowns!

We'll lounge beside my indoor pool –
Consider it your brand new school –
Stroke lovingly each satin fern
And piles and piles of greenbacks earn,

Miss May, and swarms of loving fans.
Now hurry along and make some plans
For movie shoots, you never know –
Attach your tail, watch your assets grow.

See Dick run for your autograph
When you're a member of my staff.
You'll live right here above the pool –
Gosh, you're fast – sure, just like boarding school.

Should you win Playmate of the Year
You'll score a car and much pink gear
And suntan oil, Kahlua, bike
Enough other swag to stuff a dike!

So pose for me and be my bunny –
Hear the whole world call you Honey.
Just wait and see if I'm not right –
You'll make a bundle overnight!

This is it, the primrose path.
You measure up, I've seen your math.
You've aced the dip, your future's sunny.
Now pose for me, there's a good bunny.

"And do you enjoy crafts?" the headmistress asked.
"Oh *yes*," we chorused.
"Well then, let's get busy, girls!"
Mounds of sequins and turkey feathers
and fringe and rhinestones and pigeon fluff and
glue and thread and velvet quilt patches and bugle beads
and darning needles on the Formica table then girdles
and aprons and D-cup brassieres garter belts from the Sally Ann
and shiny parts of cast-off skating costumes and tassels galore
and while the wheat turned to its gold shimmy
we bent to our work.

"And have you girls read *Frankenstein*," the headmistress queried.
"Of course," we chorused, blissful, stitching sequins to aprons,
feathers to girdles, velvet to garters. She explained our outfits
would spring from old scraps and come alive like the monster, only
happier.

When the village people heard they seized all our glittering handiwork.
They fired the headmistress in a puff of iridescent smoke.
They built a great bonfire and circled it, smacking their lips
as if they'd dine on the flames.

We seek the vintage stars, headliners of last
century, mothers of the art, empresses of the stage,
showgirls with cheeks cracked like staves in fans,
sprung joints, loose noodles of flesh like G-strings
stranded on a clothesline. Bette Davis eyes. Wattled
minds in some cases. We just want to share
the same room, hear the stories (no matter how
sideways), discover whiffs of worlds past,
the source for premium ostrich feathers, secrets
of fan-grasps. The ultimate reveal.
Tricky to track down vintage virtuosos –
they've reverted to their real names, Ada, Betty.
The phone book no use at all, no listing
for Sugarpuss O'Shea. We sleuths in corsets
will comb the continent if that's what
it takes. Follow instinct, hunch, glint of rhinestone
in a trailer-park window, trampled tassel
in a back alley, in one or two cases of wild success,
a ranch with diamond-studded stallions.
To take me trick-or-treating my mother once
dressed as a gypsy. How much she enjoyed her
costume alarmed me at the time. I was young.
Our old mothers, found, fetch scrapbooks,
creak them open, brittle news clippings, pages
that shutter as ancient hands
turn them   ever   so   slow.

While we watched the famous American comic mimic seagulls
Harpies drank martinis. Harpies drank bourbon.
Harpies knew nostalgia is futile. Harpies hunted quails.
Seagulls, look out! Miss July might mistake you for a quail.
Bunnies, beware! She declares coastal rock formations
Turn her on. She feels at home surrounded by rocks.
She eschews the eggheads and bores, the whole
Binky and Buzzy set. Nature is her groove, her pet
Ocelot. She calls herself too emotional
To be a divorce lawyer ("I'd always side with the men").
If she were a poet she'd capitalize the first word
Of every line. We didn't know any poets or harpies
Or divorced people, only a few shacked-up souls.
Guileless as seagulls, we'd feed our eyes on any scrap at all.

The farm dripped with sex. A farm always does. Nothing can
staunch those fields against sex. And the house? As a garrison the
house is a joke. Witness the peonies loosing themselves in the doily
crevices, Harpies. No embroidery, not even the deftest needle, can
fortress a farm. A farm will leak no matter what, it will leak sex.
The bible on the piano decrees it. Bible-Land had its orgies, too,
older men, many women. Jellied salads melt in the face of sex and
yes sex has a face but most of all it bounces. Look at the televised
girls on *Hee Haw*, how they bounce and the chorus girls owned
by Ziegfeld before them. A farm has been called the middle of
nowhere but it's no Void-ville! Things work their way in. How we
strove to mime that *Hee Haw* bounce; we didn't even know one
of its bounciest ladies was Hugh Hefner's girlfriend. We lopped
off our denim jeans, shrunk them to resemble Elly May on *The
Beverly Hillbillies* (how she'd bounce beside the cement pond –
oil and money and sex!). Outdoors, a steady gush of sex all day
long. The blunderous mounting bull. A rooster's quick crude ride.
Piercing dives of bees into buckwheat, supper, intercourse all at once
(flowering crops a model of efficiency). Sex thrown high in the shape
of bales, bare-chested brawny neighbour boys loading hay, yaw
of muscle and flex. Sex. Winter's snowplow driver, his great white
ejaculating spray.

My tray loaded with highballs, shaking in my teenage hands.
The Cardinal Motor Hotel on Highway 6 closest thing to a Playboy
Club in those parts. Exotica. Hot Beef Dip, red tablecloths. The
lounge with its dark panelling, swag lamps. And the motel? Sin
Central, travellers southbound to board a plane at Malton. *To the
southward, Fergus and Guelph were on the fringes of civilization.
From that fringe, a finger-thrust of civilization – the Garafraxa
Road – had been pierced northwestward by the Government of
Upper Canada.* Or northbound. *To the northward, the Georgian
Bay stretched its length along the lonely shores of Grey and Bruce
and bathed the rocky and silent beaches of the Indian Peninsula.*
I waitressed somewhere near the knuckle, partway up the finger-
thrust. *Was* a knucklehead, never getting drink orders straight.
The first settlers of Grey and Bruce were men of iron vigour. The
descendants of the men of iron drank Export Ale when alone. With
ladies they still drank Export Ale. The ladies, Whiskey Sour, Gimlet,
Singapore Sling. Sometimes a local politician and his wife dined at
the Cardinal. If they sat in my section I had to look sharp said my
boss, the only man with a Hungarian accent in the Queen's Bush.
Smile, he'd command in his Dracula voice, *and shorten that skirt.*
The politician's hair was cut for success and my fervent hope was
someday I'd brag I served supper to the Prime Minister. Own my
own little piece of history.

Outside the walk-in freezer hung great hulking pendulums of hides,
roasts. Sometimes a raw-boned customer made me literally cry.
Sob beside the hanging beef.

Highway 6 furled north like a Baptist goad to a reputed-racy tangle
of sand shores, Sauble, Wasaga. With only my apron and bicycle I
never got there, settled for the tear-shaped pond behind the Cardinal,
a microscopic beach. Little sand is required to instill a sensation of

wildness and after my shift for Dracula I'd don a bikini, let the sun redden me beside that provincial watering hole in an era so literal, *bush* meant bush.

(All Canadian girls have, at one time or another, roughed it in the bush, worked at a Playboy Club whether they knew it or not. Whether they wore ears and tail or not. Maybe Gloria Steinem was right, all women are bunnies.)

Waitress. Hostess. Cheerleader. Majorette. Stewardess. Candystriper. Metre maid. Honey-bunny.

At the very last minute Hefner erased the antlers, replaced them with bunny ears. At the very moment, perhaps, watchers in the Queen's Bush adjusted the rabbit ears on their televisions. Strain less to see through the snow.

JUNE ST. CLAIR'S TRAVELLERS' GUIDE FOR BURLESQUE ARTISTS, NEVER WRITTEN (CIRCA 1947)

Travel with your mother or your sister or a dog.
Post money to your brother back home. Invent
a name – after all, who'd pay to see a girl
called "Geraldine" remove her clothes?
The Platinum Princess a.k.a. June St. Clair –
now that's more *like* it! Whatever town,
go to confession. Pull a supple hat down
over your face, attend mass. Stay Catholic,
a scheme with more to look forward to afterwards.
Keep a Mary figurine in every hotel room.
Remember your origins, chickens
scratching in the yard. Lowly coat-check-girl gig,
your father in the shoe factory then not.
Imagine ascent. Never abandon Hollywood hopes.
Keep your head. Not wise to slag stars
like Gypsy Rose Lee (never let the cocktails talk).
Tick-tock a pocketful of rocks. A walk by the quarry.
Somehow your mother and sister left behind –
where's the damned dog when you need him?
You've got the drift – travel is the chronicle
of your sins, the wrong-turn map of your mistakes.
Manhattan hotel room, letter opener no longer
wants to be a letter opener. Gloves so drawn out
they could fashion a noose. A pen that writes
in a hand that once belonged to you – *I'm sorry, goodbye.*

With her armloads of flowers and leaves Anne brought burlesque to Green Gables. Pastoral burlesque. Not to mention puffed sleeves. Hyperbole. "The Lady of Shalott." A sinking boat rendered romantic. The amethyst brooch episode masqueraded as a lesson in telling the truth; really, it was a lament for the sparkly lost.

*

Farm wives, too, had their burlesque moments. My mother could juggle tangerines. Tangerines appeared in December, value-added glamour to her act. Not to mention those silver icicles swanking the Christmas trees throughout our township. Even in her ninetieth year my mother could recite long passages of Pauline Johnson.

*

The cutting gardens of rural Ontario. Federations of roses slumped over trellises. Buckets of lilacs. Butterflies and the farm dogs nipping the fragrant air, running, always running.

*

Years later I read Pauline Johnson changed into or out of her Indian princess costume partway through her act, then into or out of her Victorian lady getup, how she thrilled English audiences, O Exotic Canada. Simple as changing a dress.

*

If only they'd taught us something useful in Home Economics or Canadian Girls in Training, like making pasties or ostrich feather fans.

*

Everything is burlesque. Céline Dion. Liberace. Pigeons in a certain light. "Lady of Shalott." The Muppets. Don Cherry.

Once, before milk quotas, the bachelors had their own mansions, grand old Ontario stone, brick, gingerbread-trimmed. Inherited from pioneer parents. The sons who never moved out, the boys next door. Thirty? Forty? Fifty? Hard to tell under all that crop-scruff. Only peeks we got inside their houses – Halloween, in our masks and cardboard horse costumes, even then the narrowest peep show: kitchen linoleum, wood stove, table with oilcloth, mouldering tea bags. They might have had stacks of girly magazines in there, we never found out. Rumour was they ate soup right out of the can, a magnificent sloth, drank straight from the carton. They wore uniforms. Denim overalls. Loose like in hick cartoons. Loose men. Bodies like the scarecrow in *Wizard of Oz*. Brains? Sure. They weren't born yesterday. They were good farmers. Sometimes two shared one mansion. Queer? We never thought anything about it. They were solid neighbours with snowplows. Only once do I remember a Bush bachelor married. Wed the church pianist. He cleaned up real good.

Industrial chocolate scented their bed.
The candy factory wore her out, often
she plunged straight into a slumber Hugh
cartooned: "New Wife in Mars Wrapper"
"Still Life with Confection & Pillow"
"Milky Way, Anyone?"

She twitched like a coed on honeymoon
in Wisconsin. Her face, galvanized.
He read *Lady Chatterley's Lover*, his mother
stirring cocoa in the kitchen (highest heat
the house would reach *that* night).

He had his dreams, not always would they live
in his parents' house. His dreams: decidedly
not square. No. Effulgent, round, somehow
(he knew not yet how) animals figured in them.
Might an antlered stag, for the right price
be persuaded to don a smoking jacket,
lounge on its hind hooves, sip a martini?

Animals held the key to the future,
that much he gleaned. As for the candy lump
snoring in the other room, worthy
grist for cartoons.

People still marvel at my farm-girl appetite. Register surprise as I ravish poutine piled with two roast chickens, a pig cut in strips. They are right to marvel. It is like eating a whole farm. To this day I see salad as lost time. Rabbit food. My mother called me a bottomless pit. Formed early, our cravings are the constant haversacks we haul through life.

Never have I eaten for two but always have I eaten for history.

The piercing hungers of the past.

The pioneers of Grey and Bruce County pierced the "Bush" with roadways for settlement; cleared the forest; built schools, churches and gristmills and helped form the various municipalities. They laboured with an enthusiasm, fortitude and industry that finally overcame all obstacles. After many weary months of toil at underbrushing, chopping, logging and clearing, they finally brought the land into a condition to produce something upon which they could subsist. Miles and miles of forest lay between them and the most ordinary comforts of civilized life, and over those long difficult and weary miles every pound of the necessary supplies of food had to be carried.

Thanks to those heroes of the ravenous road, civilized life lay a mere thirty-eight miles away, Kentucky Fried Chicken. KFC, my first sexual encounter (food = sex).

We were not small people. We were strapping souls who prayed before meals. Who gave thanks, dug in.

Potatoes: foreplay.
Meat: say no more.
Pastry lattice: sheer porn.

We did not talk. Waste not. We did not waste except for gristle flung from my father's plate down to the waiting dogs. Gristle was sex for farm dogs. On the human side, chicken was good sex. Fried bologna, bad sex. Bad sex was better than no sex.

Between meals and in the space between trips to civilization thirty-eight miles away there was always the dream, the Colonel's gleaming white palace, climax
of our pioneer forebearers' fortitude and industry.

KFC (orgasm)

They pierced the bush so we could achieve the great unsaid in those parts.

Saturday night in Amherst –
wild night, wild night –
crazed flies strike
the lantern – my fingers buzz,
shadow the wall
pale tiny pipes.
I crack the centrefold
dare to wonder if dear Mr. Higginson
is viewing the same picture –
my digits
tickle the computer keys –
press *send* – soon O
soon, dear Mr. Higginson
shall plump my heart's deep moss.

Soon I'll haul the pizza-in-a-basket I ordered
up by rope, in through my window
double cheese –
wild pie, wild pie –
I'll eat it all myself, a hunger untitled
bundled and slant, my top four buttons
out of seventy-eight unhooked –
a scathing expanse of collarbone.

MANET'S CENTREFOLD

(*Luncheon on the Grass*)

Fruit scattered, bread. No one eats.
It's not a real picnic. It's a dream, double date
gone south. Paint-by-nature trees,
rough sluices of callow light, gloom-green gashes.
They are a mess. No one is paying attention.
The background woman bathing or about
to throw up. The men are into each other,
culture, leisure, privilege on the grass.
The history of art a story of inertia,
shooting the breeze. If the front woman
shed thirty pounds and lived a century later *Playboy*
could be her home. The money would be better.
And people would, for once, appreciate her
most erotic part, that prominent ear,
cocked towards the craving world beyond the frame.

His girlfriends have names like Buffy, Cristal. Crystal. Krystal.
Blonde. Flaxen. Strawberry. Platinum. He's not certain
of their names but if he calls "Crystal" someone always
comes, or a drink does, served in cut glass.
From the mansion they come and go, talking of Michelangelo.
Sometimes, when he calls "Crystal" *several* spring to his side
wagging with the obedience of well-trained dogs.
Money makes the best circus master.
Of course he's not just another rich old man.
Dolphins leap outside his window, beauty abounds.
They've invented a special drug just for him and he can
afford it by the keg. He doesn't let its blue hue put him
off and it doesn't. His big round bed grew global
years ago, a whole factory busy sewing custom-made
sheets. He keeps people in work. Besides his vast personal
archive he has a library for the rare bookish ladies
in his mansion (by *God* they look sexy
in those librarian spectacles!). As for himself
he's a walking talking history book. Show him the bunny.

A glue gun is handy to carry through life.
When sticky situations arise brandish
it declare you have a glue gun (which you do)
and you're not afraid to use it (recall all
the rifle-toting vintage Playmates).
A sack of sequins is wise, hurl handfuls
at your pursuer, a scratch-cloud of glitter,
aim for the eyes. A large ostrich fan
doubles as a shrub to hide behind.
Needles. Never leave home without them.
A generous swatch of illusion fabric.
Spirit gum. Fishnets. Never know when company
will drop in, be ready at the trout stream
with tackle and net. Sing to the fish,
fish like Prince. Wear breakaway pants.
When the night sky is shot through
with comets grommets rhinestone stars
shaped like kitchen pots or at the next
harvest moon un-tug your corset laces
soundly, in an open direction, release.

Elbow gloves floored in smouldering folds,
fingers hollow, spent and splayed.
The poet, bare-armed, winks at the reader
decked out, as always, in illusion fabric.
And now this little book is done.

Curtains.

NOTES ON THE POEMS

The first epigraph comes from John Donne's poem "To His Mistress Going to Bed" (Elegy 8). Donald R. Dickson, ed., *John Donne's Poetry* (New York: W.W. Norton, 2007), 35.

The second epigraph is taken from "A Substance in a Cushion" by Gertrude Stein. *Tender Buttons* (Mineola, New York: Dover Publications, 1997), 4.

"A Rose for Yvette Vickers (1928–2010 or 2011)" owes a debt to William Faulkner's short story "A Rose for Emily."

The epigraph to "Zorita" is taken from Liz Goldwyn's book, *Pretty Things: The Last Generation of American Burlesque Queens* (New York: HarperCollins Publishers, 2006), 259.

The epigraph to "There's Always a Mansion" comes from Lynn Crosbie's novel, *Dorothy L'Amour* (Toronto: HarperFlamingo Canada, 1999).

The first stanza of italicized text of "Landscape with Various Voyeurs" is taken from F. Scott Fitzgerald's *The Great Gatsby*, that magnificent poetic meditation, in novel form, on loneliness.

The epigraph to "A Swinger's Guide to London" comes from *Playboy*, December 1966.

"Lament for the Sparkly Lost" is for Wendy Roy.

ACKNOWLEDGEMENTS

In addition to numerous *Playboy* magazines and several books on Hugh Hefner and the Playboy empire, the following sources were useful: Becki L. Ross' *Burlesque West: Showgirls, Sex, and Sin in Postwar Vancouver* (Toronto: University of Toronto Press, 2009); Liz Goldwyn's *Pretty Things: The Last Generation of American Burlesque Queens* (New York: HarperCollins Publishers, 2006); Jo Weldon's *Burlesque Handbook* (New York: HarperCollins Publishers, 2010); Rachel Shteir's *Striptease: The Untold History of the Girlie Show* (New York: Oxford University Press, 2004); Michelle Baldwin's *Burlesque and the New Bump-n-Grind* (Denver: Speck Press, 2004). The documentary films *Hugh Hefner: Playboy, Activist and Rebel*, directed by Brigitte Berman (Toronto: Phase 4 Films, 2010) and *Behind the Burly Q*, directed by Leslie Zemeckis (New York: First Run Features, 2010) provided lively perspectives and venerable footage. A final key source was W. M. Brown's *The Queen's Bush: A Tale of the Early Days of Bruce County* (London, ON: John Bale, Sons & Danielsson, Ltd, 1932).

About a half-dozen of these poems were first read at Kingston WritersFest's SpeakEasy in 2011. Thanks to the musicians who set the poems to music and to the festival's Artistic Director, Merilyn Simonds, for the opportunity to try out these poems in a live-performance venue.

"The Oldest Living Swinger in Canada" was first published in the anthology *That Not Forgotten,* edited by Bruce Kauffman (Brighton, ON: Hidden Brook Press, 2012). Further thanks to Bruce Kauffman for providing a space to read this poem at his monthly Artel Reading Series in Kingston, ON. "Thinking of You during Security Screening at Calgary Airport" first appeared in the anthology *Pith and Wry: Canadian Poetry*, edited by Susan McMaster (Sudbury, ON: Scrivener Press, 2010).

Grand thanks to Jackie Latendresse for a terrific burlesque class at Free Flow Dance in Saskatoon, and to all the sparkly ladies who shared laughter, mirrors and spirit gum.

Several early poems allegedly about canoes opened a space for sexual themes in Canadian poetry. Lorna Crozier and Robert Kroetsch carried forward this possibility – unreserved thanks to the pioneers and carriers-on.

Thanks to everyone in the Department of English at the University of Saskatchewan for providing such a collegial environment in which to finish this book; special thanks to Lisa Vargo and Hilary Clark. Thanks, too, to everyone at the Interdisciplinary Centre for Culture and Creativity at the University of Saskatchewan, in particular, LaVina Watts. Sabrina Kehoe's shoes are muses in the workplace. Matthew Hall, thanks for the engaging chats about writing and poetics. I'm grateful to Carole Capling for giving me a copy of *The Queen's Bush*. Andrew Stubbs sourced me some vintage *Playboys* in Regina in 2008. Much gratitude to my excellent editor, Roo Borson; that's a mighty fine fine-toothed comb she's got. Above all, love and thanks to Roger Dorey.